POEMS TWICE TOLD

Regards to Roberta Russell
Jay Macpherson
8. iii. 76.

Jay Macpherson
POEMS TWICE TOLD
The Boatman & Welcoming Disaster

Toronto
OXFORD UNIVERSITY PRESS
1981

For Norrie as always

Canadian Cataloguing in Publication Data

Macpherson, Jay, 1931-
   Poems twice told

Originally published as two separate works: The
Boatman. Toronto : Oxford, 1957, and, Welcoming
disaster. Toronto : Saannes Publications, 1974.
ISBN 0-19-540379-7

I. Title.

PS8525.P53P63   C811' .54   C81-095020-0
PR9199.3.M3367P63

© Oxford University Press Canada 1981
ISBN 0-19-540379-7
2 3 4 - 7 6 5
Printed in Canada by John Deyell Limited

CONTENTS

CONTENTS

CONTENTS

THE BOATMAN

NO MAN'S NIGHTINGALE

Sir, no man's nightingale, your foolish bird,
I sing and thrive, by Angel finger fed,
And when I turn to rest, an Angel's word
Exalts an air of trees above my head,
Shrouds me in secret where no single thing
May envy no-man's-nightingale her spring.

I

POOR CHILD

ORDINARY PEOPLE IN THE LAST DAYS

My mother was taken up to heaven in a pink cloud.
She was talking to a friend on the telephone
When we saw her depart through the ceiling
Still murmuring about bridge.

My father prophesied.
He looked out from behind his newspaper
And said, 'Johnny-Boy will win the Derby'.
The odds against were fifteen to one, and he won.

The unicorn yielded to my sweetheart.
She was giggling with some girls
When the unicorn walked carefully up to her
And laid his head in her lap.

The white bull ran away with my sister.
My father sent me to find her
But the oracle maundered on about a cow
And I came home disgruntled.

The dove descended on my brother.
He was working in the garden
When the air became too bright for comfort
And the glory of the bird scorched his roses.

A mouse ran away in my wainscot.
I study all day and pray all night.
My God, send me a sign of Thy coming
Or let me die.

My mother was taken up to heaven in a pink cloud,
My father prophesied,
The unicorn yielded to my sweetheart,
The white bull ran away with my sister,
The dove descended on my brother.
And a mouse ran away in my wainscot.

POOR CHILD

The child is mortal; but Poor Child
Creeps through centuries of bone
Untransient as the channelling worm
Or water making sand of stone.
Poor child, what have they done to you?

Poor child the royal goosegirl combing
Her hair in the field: poor children too
Achilles sulking, Odysseus returned,
Philoctetes, Prufrock, and you and you.
Poor child, what have they done to you?

Go farther back: for these poor children,
Ruined from the womb, still yearn
To swing in dark or water, wanting
Not childhood's flowers but absolute return.
Poor child, what have we done?

THE THREAD

Each night I do retrace
My heavy steps and am compelled to pass
To earlier places, but take up again
The journey's turning skein.

The thread Night's daughters spin
Runs from birth's dark to death's, a shining line.
The snipping Fate attends its end and mine,
Ends what the two begin.

My mother gave to lead
My blind steps through the maze a daedal thread.
Who slept, who wept on Naxos now star-crowned
Reigns she whom I disowned.

The ceaseless to and from
Hushes the cry of the insatiate womb
That I wind up the journey I have come
And follow it back home.

THE THIRD EYE

Of three eyes, I would still give two for one.
The third eye clouds: its light is nearly gone.
The two saw green, saw sky, saw people pass:
The third eye saw through order like a glass
To concentrate, refine and rarify
And make a Cosmos of miscellany.
Sight, world and all to save alive that one
Fading so fast! Ah love, its light is done.

COLD STONE

I lay my cheek against cold stone
And feel my self returned to me
As soft my flesh and firm my bone
By it declare their quality.
I hear my distant blood drive still
Its obscure purpose with clear will.

The stone's unordered rigour stands
Remote and heavy as a star.
My returned self in cheek and hands
Regards as yet not very far
The leap from shape to living form;
For where I rested, the stone is warm.

IN TIME OF PESTILENCE

She is sick: and shall she heal?
Well she may, the world is foul.

What comfort shall those hands afford
That fondled Typhon's new-born head?
What good charm shall that throat record
Stabbed through to keep her in her bed?

Shall mercy cloud the shining breast
That lights the water as it drives?
And who, enfranchised to her rest,
Once stirs his slept-out head, revives?

It is her work her child lies dead,
Her voice the heights of mourning scales:
Not by her will the severed head
Sings in a grove of nightingales.

She is sick: and shall she heal?
Well she may, the world is foul.

SHE

She who is fickle sea
And indifferent sky
Is that clear star men flee
These dangers by.

Thus I know this of you:
You will be labyrinth, and clue.

TRUE NORTH

All other winters shall break against hers,
Such fire is wedded to her frost.
She is harsh as the blizzard that scrapes and strains,
Firm as the mountains, crowned as the firs,
Rich as the earth's old smouldering veins,
And to the level mild world locked and lost.

THE BLIGHTED SPRING

Over her dominion rests
A stagnant air that blasts but cannot blow.
Her orchards are devoured with pests,
The very suckers will not grow.
—Yet in her trees how green and hopeful nests
The industrious mistletoe!

THE ILL WIND

To reply, in face of a bad season,
Pestilential cold, malignity,
To the ill wind weeping on my shoulder,
'Child, what have I to do with thee?'

Is to deny the infant head
And the voice complaining tirelessly:
'Is there room for one only under your cloak,
Mother, may I creep inside and see?
Did you not know my wicked will
When you summoned me?'

II

O EARTH RETURN

A SPECULUM FOR FALLEN WOMEN

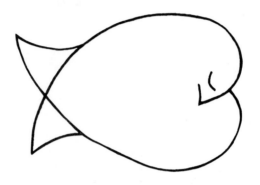

EVE IN REFLECTION

Painful and brief the act. Eve on the barren shore
Sees every cherished feature, plumed tree, bright grass,
Fresh spring, the beasts as placid as before
Beneath the inviolable glass.

There the lost girl gone under sea
Tends her undying grove, never raising her eyes
To where on the salt shell beach in reverie
The mother of all living lies.

The beloved face is lost from sight,
Marred in a whelming tide of blood:
And Adam walks in the cold night
Wilderness, waste wood.

SIBYLLA

Who questions now, who offers thanks, who grieves?
No memory lingers
In the sand I run between my fingers,
In the whirling leaves.

Where is your god, Sibylla? where is he
Who came in other days
To lay his bright head on your knee
And learn the secrets of Earth's ways?

Silence: the bat-clogged cave
Lacks breath to sigh.
Sibylla, hung between earth and sky,
Sways with the wind in her pendant grave.

EURYNOME

In the snake's embrace mortal she lies,
Dies, but lives to renew her torment,
Under her, rock, night on her eyes.
In the wall around her was set by One
Upright, staring, to watch for morning
With bread and candle, her little son.

THE RYMER

When leaves and rain together fall
And you lie cold and sleep
As if your hollow bed were all,
What should I do but weep?

Under the dead grove like seed lying,
A forest knotted in your hair,
Hands slack, face hidden, unreplying,
Buried too deep for care—

O turn to me! the fruit is rotten
That shone so red and green,
And still I harp and carp: but you have forgotten,
Love, what I mean.

LOVE IN EGYPT

Love, here are thorns, and here's a wilderness
—And yet you visit me?
I have a cell, your rod—
No more to see.

A spring restores these sands,
Pouring its rocky basin full.
Love, will you drink from my hands,
Or rather from my skull?

SHEBA

One the cruel Sun embraced, on whom he laid his brand
Black but come-hitherly, with gold in her hand,
The King of Egypt's daughter, came to visit me,
And all for the sake of my little burning tree.

I have a little sister far undersea,
The winds and the waters bring her words to me:
'True love is a durable fire the floods shall not drown.'
The bird sings burning and on her branch sinks down.

THE MARRIAGE OF EARTH AND HEAVEN

Earth draws her breath so gently, heaven bends
On her so bright a look, I could believe
That the renewal of the world was come,
The marriage of kind Earth and splendid Heaven.

'O happy pair'—the blind man lifts his harp
Down from the peg—but wait, but check the song.
The two you praise still matchless lie apart,
Thin air drawn sharp between queen Earth and Heaven.

Though I stand and stretch my hands forever
Till my hair grows down my back and my skirt to my ankles,
I shall not hear the triumphs of their trumpets
Calling the hopeful in from all the quarters
To the marriage of kind Earth and splendid Heaven.

Yet out of reason's reach a place is kept
For great occasions, with a fat four-poster bed
And a revelling-ground and a fountain showering beer
And a fiddler fiddling fine for folly's children
To riot rings around at the famous wedding
Of quean Earth and her fancy-fellow Heaven.

THE SWAN

White-habited, the mystic Swan
Walks her rank cloister as the night draws down,
In sweet communion with her sister shade,
Matchless and unassayed.

The tower of ivory sways,
Gaze bends to mirrored gaze:
This perfect arc embraces all her days.
And when she comes to die,
The treasurers of her silence patent lie:
'I am all that is and was and shall be,
My garment may no man put by.'

THE DAY-LABOURER

Time is a labourer on God's farm,
And keeps His living things from harm.
He sees the fledglings on the bough
And wards the serpent from their nest;
He leads the Unicorn to plow,
At evening brings him home to rest:
The eternal Phoenix on his arm
Roosts, rustling the warm feathers of her breast.

III

THE PLOWMAN IN DARKNESS

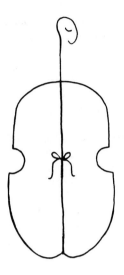

Take not that Spirit from me
That kindles and inspires,
That raises world from water,
The phoenix from her fires,
Stirs up the ravaged nightingale
To bloom among her briars.

Sweet Spirit, Comforter
That raises with a word
The swallow in her house of mud,
True but absurd,
Allow a babbling bird.

SIBYLLA

God Phoebus was a merry lad,
Courted my mother's daughter:
Said I, 'To swim I'll be quite glad,
But keep me from the water.'

He swore he'd break my looking-glass
And dock my maiden tresses;
He told me tales of many a pass,
All of them successes.

There's other ways to catch a god
Who's feeling gay and girly
Than tickling with a fishing-rod
Among the short and curly.

I took his gift and thwarted him,
I listened to his vows, and
Though looks are gone and eyes grow dim,
I'll live to be a thousand.

I'm mercifully rid of youth,
No callers plague me ever:
I'm virtuous, I tell the truth—
And you can see I'm clever!

EURYNOME

Come all old maids that are squeamish
And afraid to make mistakes,
Don't clutter your lives up with boyfriends:
The nicest girls marry snakes.

If you don't mind slime on your pillow
And caresses as gliding as ice
—Cold skin, warm heart, remember,
And besides, they keep down the mice—

If you're really serious-minded,
It's the best advice you can take:
No rumpling, no sweating, no nonsense,
Oh who would not sleep with a snake?

THE RYMER

Hear the voice of the Bard!
Want to know where I've been?
Under the frost-hard
Ground with Hell's Queen,
Whom there I embraced
In the dark as she lay,
With worms defaced,
Her lips gnawed away
—What's that? Well, maybe
Not everybody's dame,
But a sharp baby
All the same.

MARY OF EGYPT

Little children, gather round
On this bare and stony ground,
Listen while your tired and hoary
Mother tells a bed-time story.

In a far-off former time
And a green and gentle clime,
Mamma was a lively lass,
Liked to watch the tall ships pass,
Loved to hear the sailors sing
Of sun and wind and voyaging,
Felt a wild desire to be
On the bleak and unplowed sea.
Mamma was a nice girl, mind,
Hard up, but a good sport and kind—
Well, the blessed upshot was,
Mamma worked her way across
From Egypt to the Holy Land,
And here repents, among the sand.

THE ARK

Cock-robin and the jenny-wren,
The eagle and the lark,
The cuckoo and the broody-hen,
The heavens did remark
Consorting in the Ark:

The pelican in her piety,
The peacock in his pride,
Cormorant insatiety,
The feather-breasted bride,
All bedded down inside.

There sat upon the hatch-lid
The turtle and the crow.
One I've heard the Flood did,
One the Fire shall, o'erthrow
—Not in our lifetime, though.

HAIL WEDDED LOVE!

Oh the many joys of a harlot's wedding,
Countless as the ticks that tumble in the bedding!
All knives are out and slicing fast,
The bread-oven goes with a furnace-blast,
Drink flows like sea-water, cock crows till dawn,
The children of Bedlam riot in the corn.

The nymphs of Bridewell leave their fountains
To come and dance on the blockish mountains,
The meadow shoots cuckoo-pint all over
And Venus-flytrap common as clover,
The goat-shagged fiddler with urgent bow
Drives on the measure of boot and toe,
The bridegroom woos, 'My bird, my cunny,
My jam, my pussy, my little pot of honey—'

Well, delight attend their pillow!
And I'll go seek a bending willow
To hang my silent harp upon
Beside the river of Babylon.

ISIS

I'm Isis of Saïs,
If you'd know what my way is,
Come riddle my riddle-mi-ree.
It's perfectly easy
For those who're not queasy—
Say, am I a he or a she?
There's no-one shall wed me
And least of all bed me,
In fact no-one loves me but me:
Aha, you don't know? you
'd prefer me to show you?
The answer will slay you, you'll see!

O FENIX CULPA

The wicked Phoenix in her baleful fires
Here on this ground suspires.
What God has put asunder here combines
And viprish intertwines.
Duplicity of head and heart
Has taught her lust that art.
Not strength and sweetness in one frame,
Dying and rising still the same:
Her charnel and her marriage-bed,
The womb that her own being bred
—Strains to rise and cannot fly,
Looks to death and may not die,
Writhes on griefs beyond recall
And shall, till doomfire burn all.

THE PLOWMAN IN DARKNESS

You ask for the Plowman:
He's as much
In the dark as you are.
Moves by touch,
Stubbing his toes
From age to age
Is working up a
Snorting rage,
Swears he'll beat his plowshare
Into a sword
Come the great and harrowing
Day of the Lord.

While Philomel's unmeasured grief
Poured out in barren waste
Raises a tree in flower and leaf
By angel guardian graced,

Her sister, snug in walls of clay,
Performs as she is able:
Chatters, gabbles, all the day,
Raises both Cain and Babel.

IV

THE SLEEPERS

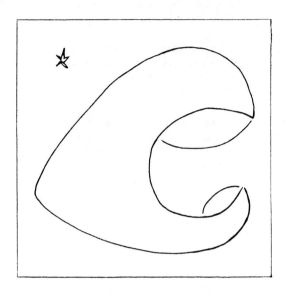

THE GARDEN OF THE FALL

The garden where the little king
Contemplates his loves in stone,
Breathless, branching, in a ring,
All for his delight alone,

Has other treasures gleaming bright:
Wounded trees that bleed and weep;
Peacocks like a starry night
Whose weary watchers dare not sleep;

A fountain rising, glittering, tall,
Whose colonnades of ice enthrall
Cruel king, proud birds, and all,
Mirrored in the water's fall.

THE SLEEPING SHEPHERD

The gold day gone, now Lucifer
Lights shepherds from the eastern hill.
The air grows sharp, the grasses stir.
One lies in slumber sunken still.

Oh wake him not until he please,
Lest he should rise to weep:
For flocks and birds and streams and trees
Are golden in his silver sleep.

THE LUNATIC SHEPHERD

Saw you not my true love
By the way as you came?
He is strayed from his wits and himself,
From his home and his name

To follow all the long night
Another one than me,
Her pale feet in the pathless wood,
Her white face on the sea.

Suppose his joy is that she
Of whom our elders say
She has power to entrance whom she will
And to ravish away,

Then I that am flesh and blood
And aching hollow bone
In dim night and dense wood
Wander these ways alone

Weary for one who lies still
In slumber sound on Latmos hill.

THE WOUNDED SHEPHERD

Involved and dim, the shepherd in his wound
As sun in branches towards evening held,
Lies without pain, by no desire impelled,
His body slack upon the chilling ground.

Waxing and waning, moved by love and grief,
His friend keeps useless watch; for nothing may
Approach their rest, not death nor waking day.
The wide wound drinks her tears without relief.

His flock strays helpless on the fearful height,
Her lamp has guttered in the hollow grave.
Below, above, the interlunar cave
Surrounds them in one ever-lasting night.

THE MARTYRS

The sexes waking, now separate and sore,
Enjoy conjunction not feasible before;
But never long enough, never near enough, nor yet
Find their death mortal, however deeply met.

Bound to cross-purposes, transfixed with desire,
His raw heart unsheltered behind its broken wall,
The first martyr bleeds impaled upon the briar
Whose root is pleasure's spring, whose arms are sorrow's fall.

The woman meanwhile sits apart and weaves
Red rosy garlands to dress her joy and fear.
But all to no purpose; for petals and leaves
Fall everlastingly, and the small swords stand clear.

THE GARDEN OF THE SEXES

I have a garden closed away
And shadowed from the light of day
Where Love hangs bound on every tree
And I alone go free.

His sighs, that turn the weathers round,
His tears, that water all the ground,
His blood, that reddens in the vine,
These all are mine.

At night the golden apple-tree
Is my fixed station, whence I see
Terrible, sublime and free,
My loves go wheeling over me.

AIAIA

Now from the sanctified island the light descending
With wailing into the dark
Leaves the live tree, the mothers harsh and bending,
The bridebed closed in bark,

Declines, slips fast through the blackened air
Till the cruel deceiver, gentle at last,
Dawns on extinguished eyes whose stars are past,
Laps the fond innocent head in her cradle of care.

THE UNICORN-TREE

Bound and weeping, but with smiles
To keep herself from scorn,
The lady of the tree beguiles
The wrathful unicorn.

What anger in the springing wood
Or coil along the bough
Flushes the milky skin with blood?
Too late to question now.

The hunters with their kill are gone.
The darkening tree again
Arches its wicked length upon
The virgin in her chain.

THE OLD ENCHANTER

The old enchanter who laid down his head
In woman's mazeful lap was not betrayed
By love or doting, though he gave a maid
His rod and book and lies now like the dead.

The world's old age is on us. Long ago,
Shaken by dragons, swamped with sea-waves, fell
The island fortress, drowned like any shell.
This dreamer hears no tales of overthrow,

In childish sleep brass-walled by his own charms.
In Merlin's bosom Arthur and the rest
Sleep their long night; and Arthur's dragon crest
Seems pacified, though in a witch's arms.

THE LAND OF NOD

Cain since first he fled
Is endless bound to run
Under a scorching sun
That burns a baneful red,

Or hunt among cold rocks
And stiffened marble streams.
Only in Abel's dreams
The crushing wheel unlocks.

For Abel's sake, the dead
Shepherd dear to God,
Cain in the Land of Nod
Covers his dreadful head.

Where Abel, cheek on hand,
Sleeps his silver night,
An arky moon makes bright
Calm sheepfolds, quiet land;

And while his brother's keeper
Lies so near God's heart,
There shall no judgment fall to part
Sleeper from sleeper.

THE FAITHFUL SHEPHERD

Cold pastoral: the shepherd under the snow
Sleeps circled with his sheep.
Above them though successive winters heap
Rigours, and wailing weathers go
Like beasts about, time only rocks their sleep,
An ark upon a deep.
And drowsy care, to keep a world from death,
Maintains his steady heartbeat and warm breath.

THE SECRET SLEEPER

His sleep sustains the golden tree,
His night the shining day,
His calm the turtle on her nest,
His rest the fountain-spray.

He need not ask for whose delight
His flowering dreams will rise,
Nor buried in what crystal breast
He securely lies.

THE CAVERNED WOMAN

What's packed about her ivory bones
Is cruel to the wondering touch;
Her hard skull rounds the roots of stones
And cannot give or comfort much;

Her lap is sealed to summer showers,
Ice-bound, and ringed in iron hold:
Her breast puts forth its love like flowers
Astonished into hills of cold.

Not here the Sun that frees and warms,
Cherishes between fire and flood:
But far within are Seraph forms,
Are flowers, fountains, milk, blood.

HELEN

While Helen slept in Egypt, the cruel war
Roared, lashed and swallowed, spat up broken men.
But she knew nothing of this, lying withdrawn
Far by the heaven-fed river, the holy stream.

Her beauty unshadowed upon the bearing land
Rests like a seal. Unharvested, unsown
Its seeds lie folded, waiting in her hand.
Her patience guards the desert, her great repose in stone.

PSYCHE

My house long quiet, every hearthstone chill
And dust upon the sill:
No tremor in its somnolence or spark
Through-chinking comes to mark
Where Psyche sets her candle in my night
Or who regards that light.

THE INNOCENTS

Bloody, and stained, and with mothers' cries,
These silly babes were born;
And again bloody, again stained, again with cries,
Sharp from this life were torn.

A waste of milk, a waste of seed;
Though white the forest stands
Where Herod bleeds his rage away
And wrings his bloodless hands.

THE NATURAL MOTHER

All the soft moon bends over,
All circled in her arm,
All that her blue folds cover,
Sleeps shadowed, safe and warm.

Then lullaby King David's town,
The shepherds in the snow,
Rough instruments, uneasy crown,
And cock about to crow,

And lullaby the wakeful bird
That mourns upon the height,
The ancient heads with visions stirred,
The glimmering new light;

Long rest to purple and to pall,
The watchers on the towered wall,
The dreamland tree, the waterfall:
Lullaby my God and all.

THE NURSE

Drowsy she sits and sings, and drowsy starts to spin,
To make her nursling smile,
A sensual shining web that might beguile
The sun from heaven: but starless night within.

Murmuring and nodding so, she will not see
Her first last love bound down in swaddling bands,
Too weak to weep or stretch his infant hands,
Rocking in Adam's sleep on Adam's tree.

V

THE BOATMAN

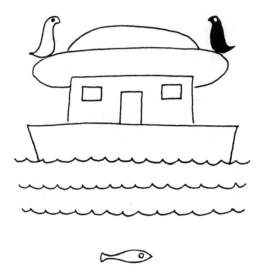

THE BOATMAN

You might suppose it easy
For a maker not too lazy
To convert the gentle reader to an Ark:
But it takes a willing pupil
To admit both gnat and camel
—Quite an eyeful, all the crew that must embark.

After me when comes the deluge
And you're looking round for refuge
From God's anger pouring down in gush and spout,
Then you take the tender creature
—You remember, that's the reader—
And you pull him through his navel inside out.

That's to get his beasts outside him,
For they've got to come aboard him,
As the best directions have it, two by two.
When you've taken all their tickets
And you've marched them through his sockets,
Let the tempest bust Creation: heed not you.

For you're riding high and mighty
In a gale that's pushing ninety
With a solid bottom under you—that's his.
Fellow flesh affords a rampart,
And you've got along for comfort
All the world there ever shall be, was, and is.

I. THE ARK

ARK TO NOAH

I wait, with those that rest
In darkness till you come,
Though they are murmuring flesh
And I a block and dumb.

Yet when you come, be pleased
To shine here, be shown
Inward as all the creatures
Drawn through my bone.

ARK ARTICULATE

Shaped new to your measure
From a mourning grove,
I am your sensing creature
And may speak for love.

If you repent again
And turn and unmade, me,
How shall I rock my pain
In the arms of a tree?

ARK ANATOMICAL

Set me to sound for you
The world unmade
As he who rears the head
In light arrayed,

That its vision may quicken
Every wanting part
Hangs deep in the dark body
A divining heart.

ARK ARTEFACT

Between me and the wood
I grew in, you stand
Firm as when first I woke
Alive in your hand.

How could you know your love,
If not defined in me,
From the grief of the always wounded,
Always closing sea?

ARK APPREHENSIVE

I am a sleeping body
Hulling down the night,
And you the dream I ferry
To shores of light.

I sleep that you may wake,
That the black sea
May not gape sheer under you
As he does for me.

ARK ASTONISHED

Why did your spirit
Strive so long with me?
Will you wring love from deserts,
Comfort from the sea?

Your dove and raven speed,
The carrion and the kind.
Man, I know your need,
But not your mind.

ARK OVERWHELMED

When the four quarters shall
Turn in and make one whole,
Then I who wall your body,
Which is to me a soul,

Shall swim circled by you
And cradled on your tide,
Who was not even, not ever,
Taken from your side.

ARK PARTING

You dreamed it. From my ground
You raised that flood, these fears.
The creatures all but drowned
Fled your well of tears.

Outward the fresh shores gleam
Clear in new-washed eyes.
Fare well. From your dream
I only shall not rise.

II. THE ISLAND

THE CREATURE ESSENTIAL

The creature essential and necessary,
Lucid in private light,
Creator cloud-hung, dispensable,
Gone away into night:

My sensible sun, joy radical,
Dear Spirit, world or man,
Irradiate, illumine, make me shine
As you do—if you can.

THE ISLAND

No man alone an island: we
Stand circled with a lapping sea.
I break the ring and let you go:
Above my head the waters flow.

Look inward, love, and no more sea,
No death, no change, eternity
Lapped round us like a crystal wall
To island, and that island all.

THE INWARD ANGEL

A diamond self, more clear and hard
Than breath can cloud or touch can stain,
About my wall keeps mounted guard,
Maintaining an impervious reign.

But planted as an inward eye
And nourishing my patient mould,
He's soft with sense, and round him I
Ingather sun where all was cold.

Look, inward Angel, cast your light:
My dark is crystal in your sight.

INLAND

Let fire and tempest wage around
Their ever-furious war:
The seaman far from ocean's sound
Sets up his dripping oar.

Where never mower's boot has trod
Nor sickle sheared the hours,
I'll plant you as my garden's god,
And twine you round with flowers.

LEVIATHAN

Now show thy joy, frolic in Angels' sight
Like Adam's elephant in fields of light.
There lamb and lion slumber in the shade.
Splendour and innocence together laid.

The Lord that made Leviathan made thee
Not good, not great, not beautiful, not free,
Not whole in love, not able to forget
The coming war, the battle still unmet.

But look: Creation shines, as that first day
When God's Leviathan went forth to play
Delightful from his hand. The brute flesh sleeps,
And speechless mercy all that sleeping keeps.

THE ANAGOGIC MAN

Noah walks with head bent down;
For between his nape and crown
He carries, balancing with care,
A golden bubble round and rare.

Its gently shimmering sides surround
All us and our worlds, and bound
Art and life, and wit and sense,
Innocence and experience.

Forbear to startle him, lest some
Poor soul to its destruction come,
Slipped out of mind and past recall
As if it never was at all.

O you that pass, if still he seems
One absent-minded or in dreams,
Consider that your senses keep
A death far deeper than his sleep.

Angel, declare: what sways when Noah nods?
The sun, the stars, the figures of the gods.

VI

THE FISHERMAN

A BOOK OF RIDDLES

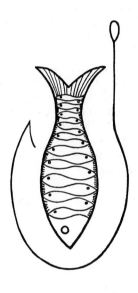

Go take the world my dearest wish
And blessing, little book.
And should one ask who's in the dish
Or how the beast was took,
Say: Wisdom is a silver fish
And Love a golden hook.

STORM

That strong creature   from before the Flood,
headless, sightless,   without bone or blood,
a wandering voice,   a travelling spirit,
butting to be born,   fierce to inherit
acreage of pity,   the world of love,
the Christian child's kingdom,   and remove
the tall towered gates   where the proud sea lay
crouched on its paws   in the first day—
came chaos again,   that outsider
would ride in,   blind steed, blind rider:
till then wails at windows,   denies relief,
batters the body   in speechless grief,
thuds in the veins,   crumples in the bone,
wrestles in darkness   and alone
for kingdoms cold,   for salt, sand, stone,
forever dispossessed.
                         Who raised this beast,
this faceless angel,   shall give him rest.

SUN AND MOON

A strong man, a fair woman,
Bound fast in love,
Parted by ordered heaven,
Punishment prove.

He suffers gnawing fires:
She in her frost
Beams in his sight, but dies
When he seems lost.

Not till the poles are joined
Shall the retreat
Of fierce brother from lost sister
End, and they meet.

WHALE

'Art thou the first of creatures, that Leviathan,
The Egyptian trickster that strives with man?'

My Maker saw his work and called me good.
I am an ark to swim the perilous flood.
With gold and spices, with candles burning sweet
In wakeful silence at his head and feet,
Vaulted in my sepulchre lies the first man,
The burden I am given to bear as I can.
I am God's creature, that Leviathan.

CORAL

A living tree that harbours
No singing-birds, no flowers,
Offers no shady arbours,
No comfortable bowers
For man's inactive hours,

The sea's untended gardens
And waving meadows bear
—A tree of flesh that hardens
In our destroying air
And stands petrific there.

It shelters shiny fishes
And leggy crustacee,
Welcomes whatever wishes,
And shines a perfect tree
Of coral in the sea.

MERMAID

The fish-tailed lady offering her breast
Has nothing else to give.
She'll render only brine, if pressed,
That none can drink and live.

She has a magic glass, whose spell
Makes bone look wondrous white.
By day she sings, though, travellers like to tell,
She weeps at night.

LUNG-FISH

The seas where once I swam as slick as herring
Are now dried up, and sunk below earth's rind.
Who lays his nets to take me now shall find
Not fish but flesh, no Friday faring.

EGG

Reader, in your hand you hold
A silver case, a box of gold.
I have no door, however small,
Unless you pierce my tender wall,
And there's no skill in healing then
Shall ever make me whole again.
Show pity, Reader, for my plight:
Let be, or else consume me quite.

MANDRAKE

The fall from man engenders me,
Rooted beneath the deadly tree.
My certain origin I show,
Single above and forked below.
Man grubs me from my peaceful sink
To aid his horrid loves, and link
My fate more strongly with his own:
Foreknowledge racks me, and I groan.

PHOENIX

If I am that bird, then I am one alone.
Father, mother, child, I am my own.
Ashes and bone of a dead life I save
And bear about with me to find a grave,
Token that my renewed and lively breath
Is kindled from a still-repeated death.
That fire is my element, consumes and lights me,
Heals and accuses and again requites me.
I feed on the dew of heaven and live without desire:
Reader, consider a life in the fire.

ABOMINABLE SNOWMAN

The guardian stalking his eternal snows
With backward tread and never any sound
Afflicts the mind with horror more profound
Than caves and chasms among which he goes.

Below the snowline flourish greedy tribes
Who run with dogs to hunt him as a beast,
Then pass his pieces round in solemn feast
Accompanied with triumph-song and gibes.

The unoffending flesh they take for meat,
The hairless palms and cheeks, the white sad face,
Are human, even found in such a place:
Too like our own the still-reluctant feet.

BOOK

Dear Reader, not your fellow flesh and blood
—I cannot love like you, nor you like me—
But like yourself launched out upon the flood,
Poor vessel to endure so fierce a sea.

The water-beetle travelling dry and frail
On the stream's face is not more slight than I;
Nor more tremendous is the ancient whale
Who scans the ocean floor with horny eye.

Although by my creator's will I span
The air, the fire, the water and the land,
My volume is no burden to your hand.

I flourish in your sight and for your sake.
His servant, yet I grapple fast with man:
Grasped and devoured, I bless him. Reader, take.

RETINA

The struggler in the net
His agon past
Through a true gate
Comes in at last,
Leaving behind him
In quite a fix
An old man's skin and bones
Cross as two sticks.

READER

My old shape-changer, who will be
Now wild, now calm, now bound, now free,
Now like a sun, and now a storm,
Now fish, now flesh, now cold, now warm,
Mercurial, dull—but sly enough
To slip my hand and wriggle off—,
I have you fast and will not let you go:
Your nature and your name I know.

THE FISHERMAN

The world was first a private park
Until the angel, after dark,
Scattered afar to wests and easts
The lovers and the friendly beasts.

And later still a home-made boat
Contained Creation set afloat,
No rift nor leak that might betray
The creatures to a hostile day.

But now beside the midnight lake
One single fisher sits awake
And casts and fights and hauls to land
A myriad forms upon the sand.

Old Adam on the naming-day
Blessed each and let it slip away:
The fisher of the fallen mind
Sees no occasion to be kind,

But on his catch proceeds to sup;
Then bends, and at one slurp sucks up
The lake and all that therein is
To slake that hungry gut of his,

Then whistling makes for home and bed
As the last morning breaks in red;
But God the Lord with patient grin
Lets down his hook and hoicks him in.

OTHER POEMS

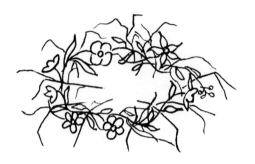

A WINTER

I

Ophelia on the threshold of the season
Stands doubting, fears, lets fall
Green love, green sorrow, shaken without reason:
Poor maiden, not the girl for fall.

II

Little sisters, brothers, go
Clean into a world of snow.
Winter builds his walls and towers
On them, and wreathes with secret flowers.
No passion breaks their age of ice,
Nor stains the white of sacrifice.

III

Artegall, Adonis red,
Azazel's malefic head,
Round us white as Abel lie,
Griefs and cruelties bled dry.
All the winter's rest receives,
But where like dirty jelly heaves
One no season's chain can free,
The strangling Adam in the sea.

LIKE ADAMANT

I thought there was no second Fall,
That I with Eve fell once for all:
But worse succeeds, I no more doubt,
Since heaven-dwellers make me out
First fallen, last obstructive grown,
Like Adamant the wounded stone.

For Adamant with Adam fell
From diamond clear to black as hell,
Though not from heaven dropped so far
As the imperious angels are,
But lies malignant in the sea,
Drawing by its infirmity.

Reader, my sound one, why should you
Hate me, or fear what I might do?
Since Adamant, as is well known,
In whom the wounds of love are shown,
Threatens the man of iron alone,
And not the man of flesh, nor stone.

THE BEAUTY OF JOB'S DAUGHTERS

The old, the mad, the blind have fairest daughters.
Take Job: the beasts the accuser sends at evening
Shoulder his house and shake it; he's not there,
Attained in age to inwardness of daughters,
In all the land no women found so fair.

Angels and sons of God are nearest neighbours,
And even the accuser may repair
To walk with Job in pleasures of his daughters:
Wide shining rooms more warmly lit at evening,
Gardens beyond whose secrets scent the air.

Not wiles of men nor envy of the neighbours,
Riches of earth, nor what heaven holds more rare,
Can take from Job the beauty of his daughters,
The gardens in the rock, music at evening,
And cup so full that all who come must share.

Perhaps we passed them? it was late, or evening,
And surely those were desert stumps, not daughters,
In fact we doubt that they were ever there.
The old, the mad, the blind have fairest daughters.
In all the land no women found so fair.

OF CREATURES THE NET

I

Of creatures the net and chain
Stretched like that great membrane
The soft sore ocean
Is by us not broken;

And like an eye or tongue
Is wet and sensing;
And by the ends drawn up
Will strain but not snap.

II

And in all natures we
The primitive he and she
Carry the child Jesus,
Those suffering senses

That in us see and taste,
With us in absence fast,
For whose scattered and bound
Sake we are joined.

III

Of the seas the wide cup
Shrinks to a water-drop,
The creatures in its round
As in an eye contained,

And that eye still the globe
Wherein all natures move,
Still tough the skin
That holds their troubles in.

IV

In all the green flood
More closely binds than blood;
Though windowed like a net
Lets none forget

The forsaken brother
And elder other;
Divided is unbroken,
Draws with the chain of ocean.

A GARDEN SHUT

A garden shut, a fountain sealed,
And all the shadowed mountains yield:
Dear Reader sits among the rocks
And fiddles at my seven locks.

How green my little world is grown
To entertain the man of stone!
The green man in the garden's lap
Draws his fill of vital sap,
But when the south wind blows is seen
Spineless as any other green.
The stone man with his burden on
Stands as stiff as Solomon,
Or wintry Herod made his heir—
Small comfort for my garden there.

The fishes in my garden's eye
Like thoughts, or thoughts like fish go by.
The crystal of the morning air
Leads up the daughters mild and fair
Closed in their bells of tinkling glass
Precious as ever Sheba was,
To gently promenade the place,
This circle of their earthly race;
Till from the shade in pride and scorn
Bursts the impetuous Unicorn,
Shatters the day and blacks the sun,
Spits rudely on his sexual thorn
The virgins one by shrieking one,
Crushes the green, and fells the stone,
Breaks fountain, wall, and so is gone.

Reader, here is no place for you.
Go wander as the wild birds do,
And never once, in peace reposed,
Wonder on whom my garden closed.

PRETTY OPHELIA!

THE WOODS NO MORE

We'll wander to the woods no more,
Nor beat about the juniper tree.
My tears run down, my heart is sore,
And none shall make a game of me.

But come, my love, another day,
I'll give you cherries with no stones,
And silver bells, and nuts in May
—But make no bones.

A WORLD OF GLASS

Sensible people as they pass
Encounter with compulsive eyes
A small damp female who applies
Nose, nipples, tummy flat against the glass
And weeps, and howls, and cries.

GIRL WITH BUCK TEETH

I am a flower
Full of stones.
Passage is offered
Between my bones.

VERY SAD SONG

I cannot claim I rise to weep,
But oh, the burden of my day
Would make an angel turn away:
I'd rather be in bed asleep.

The hurt you gave I inward keep,
Hard Love! remembering whose it is.
But rest both harm and healing his,
I'd rather be in bed asleep.

Lord, take no care my soul to keep,
For I don't need it when I sleep;
And though the host of heaven weep,
I'd rather be in bed asleep.

THE GARDENERS

My next neighbour
Worked herself to bone
Raising prize bokays
In a yard mostly stone.
I'd be rocking
On the back stoop,
And she'd say my yard
Looked like a chicken-coop.

Bet you she's raging
Over in her plot:
Nary a stalk but
Couchgrass she's got.
Can't grow nothing better
On the likes of she,
But I lie pushing daisies
Fat and white as me.

A MERMAID'S GRAVE

You who would Love's wonders see,
Pity my extremity.
He, by envy moved to intend
I should make a proper end,
Smote the waters till they boiled,
Rent my person neatly coiled,
Then, of his amusement tiring,
Cast me on green ground expiring.

Now unfeeling earth's my bed,
And round the cockle borders tread
Children, singing as they go:
'Here lies the cold mermaid, alive, alive-oh.'

TOBIT CASTING

Not the good journeying angel think
Me in your Tobit-play,
Nor Sara, but the fish: my stink
Might fright the fiend away.

THE TRAVELLER

Traveller to one Penelope,
What have you to hope from me?
But bedded in your proper West
And cuddled on connubial breast,
Forgetful, sunk past loss and pain,
Perhaps you'll see my hells again.

THE DEATH-ANGEL

You ordered me to visit him: I have.
Advised a sudden stroke: that's what he got.
You wonder he's not stinking in the grave!
Bless us, would stroking hurt him such a lot?
You can't misdoubt your faithful operative—
I only touched him lightly, Lord: he'll live.

THE LOVE-SONG OF JENNY LEAR

Come along, my old king of the sea,
Don't look so pathetic at me:
We're off for a walk
And a horrid long talk
By the beautiful banks of the sea.

I'm not Arnold's Margaret, the pearl
That gleamed and was lost in a whirl,
Who simpered in churches
And left him on porches,
But more of a hell of a girl.

Poor old fish, you're no walker at all,
Can't you spank up that elderly crawl?
I'll teach you to hurdle,
Led on by my girdle,
With whalebone, elastic and all.

We'll romp by the seashore, and when
You've enough, shut your eyes and count ten.
I'll crunch down your bones,
Guts marrow and stones,
Then raise you up dancing again.

LOVE-SONG II OF JENNY LEAR

Were I a Shakespearean daughter,
Safe restored through fire and water,
You the party in the crown
—Someone get the curtain down.

WELCOMING DISASTER

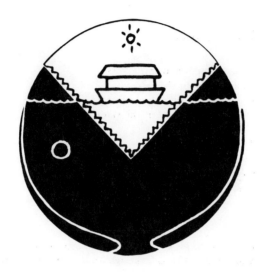

I

INVOCATIONS

POETS & MUSES

Poets are such bad employers,
Muses ought to Organize:
Time off, sick pay, danger wages—
Come, ye wretched of the skies!

Poets, to reverse the story,
Muse-redeemed, return and live:
Solomon in all his glory
Could not pay for what you give.

PS.

Breathing too is a simple trick, and most of us learn it:
Still, to lose it is bad, though no-one regrets it long.

LOST BOOKS & DEAD LETTERS

Lost the books of Gad and Enoch,
Nathan's visions, Jahweh's wars,
Lost the poets' book of Jasher:
Found, though, is the book of laws.

Lost is some of God's own story,
What he did at Arnon's brook:
But my limbs, before he formed them,
And my tears, are in his book.

Muse, with thee the book of life is,
Though my Adversary doubt:
Let me not be put to silence,
From thy page blot me not out.

HAMPSTEAD PONDS

Pools where I fished with jamjars for minnows, mysterious
Waters, linked underground, unsearchable source:
Home where I come from, well that all flow from, than memory
Deeper, the dreamland sluice that restores our friends:
Distant, sealed with a stone, but murmuring always:
If I forget thee, O secret fountain, forget not me.

THE ORACLE DECLINES

Julian Apostate, sending
Late to Delphi—'Tell the king,
Phoebus has no more his chapel,
Mantic laurel, talking spring.

Level with the ground is lying
Work of craftsmen, columned stone;
And the ever-prattling waters,
Even they are sunk and gone.'

'STILL WAITING FOR
THE SPARK FROM HEAVEN'

I meet a colleague on the stair:
He tells me of a comet:
A thing of night with streaming hair,
Of silence, of the outer air:
Shall I hope something from it?

The Magian star in bristling flight,
A Lucifer in fall:
An edgeless eye of wide affright,
With news of nothingness, of night,
If any word at all.

                    *

Come, Muse, but keep thy solitude,
Thy necessary dress:
Thy glassy distance, razor edges,
And pensive look of withered sedges—
Thy phantoms, as I guess.

Familiar oracles are dumb,
I can invoke but thee:
Approach, inviolable shade!
And scatheless as a taboo'd maid
Depart, unclutch'd by me.

No spark descends, no waters rise
Enough to wet a cheek;
And Memory, alas to me
A half-regained Eurydice,
Is veiled and cannot speak.

HOUSE LIGHTS

Lit up, the house afloat
On the dark street
Draws us: we are a crowd,
Silent, discrete.

If you put by the blind,
Left the pane free
That holds the darkness out,
What might you see—

Strangers, or denizens,
Caught on light's hook?
Or would the glass give back
Your own veiled look?

MOVIE-GOING

Welcome, darkness; welcome, silence;
Welcome, otherwordly tones:
Some approach my spirit quickens,
Entering your danger-zones.

Flickering, grey—on whose blood sated?—,
In your light what phantoms move?
Spirit at your window waits for
Angel guide or demon love.

Come, beloved, come, my saviour,
Bring me what we understand,
All I wait for: slowly rising
Coffin-lid, then skinny hand.

CONJURING THE DEAD

Conjuring the dead—who doubts it?—
Is an empty exercise.
They rise stupid, have no message,
Nothing flickers in their eyes.

Conjuring the living, maybe?
—Magic circles they decline:
Inturned, lightless, unrefractive,
Dead-engrossed, they make no sign.

Dead and living seen to meet in
Closed communion, pact profound,
Leave just where the operator?
Stupid—cumbering the ground.

ABSENCE, HAVOC

Absence, havoc—well, I missed you—
Near and dear turned far and strange,
Dayshine came disguised as midnight:
One thing altered made all change.

Fallen? stolen? trapped? entangled?
To a lower world betrayed?
Endless error held your footsteps,
On your brow a deepening shade.

Long I sought you, late I found you,
Straying on the farther shore:
You indeed? a swaying phantom
Fades, that flickered on before.
Lost, no rescue: only dreams our
Wandered, wandered loves restore.

SUBSTITUTIONS

Tedward was a
Woolworth's bear,
Filling in for
One not there
(Parents' attic?
Thrown away?
Long-dulled need re-
vived one day):
Lost the arche-
typal ted,
Friendly Tedward
Did instead.

Tedward, friend to
—Let's say—He,
Came in tow to
Visit Me:
Quaint arrangement,
I away
When this pair ar-
rived to stay.
I, returning,
Hoped to find,
Briefly, Him: no—
Left behind,
Though, was Tedward
In a chair,
Filling in for
Him not there.

Tedward, whelmed with
Spite and blame—
Lo! My Tadwit
He became:
Nose though hard and
Look though dim,
Friendly substi-
tute for Him.
Is love haunted?
To receive
What another
Needs to give
Always, somewhat,
Looked at square,
Filling in for
Those not there?

I I

THE WAY DOWN

A JOINT EPISTLE

Muses, stand easy: no high art's intended.
You help me, Tadwit: let's compose a letter
Him-wards who left you: me he still lets glimpse him, though
    Mostly in profile.

Maybe he wonders sometimes how you're keeping?
Well—you escaped the witch-doll's-den of downstairs,
Red pin in soap you passed, and since conclude you're
    Not badly treated.

What are we taking out on him this moment?
Nothing from you, my witless, that's for certain.
Searching my soul, I find a fell—, fierce—, fearsome—
    Yen to write sapphics.

                *

Could be he wonders how you got your name changed.
—Don't I hold sacred what I dimly guess at,
Child's losses, loves buried, griefs you'd call forgotten
    Only they hurt so?

Yes, fuzzpate, say I do—line jerking backwards,
Back to the cave where—Mama's breast was fuzzy?
Us did she clasp to make the pain let up some?
    Same case of razors.

He in the secret night sustains his phantoms,
Feeds from his substance, gives away his strength to,
Private, unshareable: Tadwitness, keep them.
    Me you are mine to.

FIRST & LAST THINGS

Ted, let me tell you all about the First Things,
How all that is received appointed places—
Who you and I are—and, all outside failing,
    Why we're each other's.

First was Inanna, lady of the living.
She sold to Hell, to save her skin, Dumuzi
—Child, little brother—status mixed, but most her
    First love, her shepherd.

How come a Hell, if she was first? that's easy—
Hell was Ereshkigal, her sister—her, then:
Where is he now? he had a sister too, it
    Seems, Geshtinanna:

She, skilled in words, in dreams, and self-forgetful,
Offered herself for him—he let her do it—
Flutes played, Inanna ran his this-year's bath, laid
    Out his rebirth suit.

Four, are there? No, my ted, I guess just us two:
All of those ladies I am—so my mother
Was before me: you, doll and god, my first love
    —Last, too, most likely.

SOME GHOSTS & SOME GHOULS

While we loved those who never read our poems,
Answered our letters, said the simple things we
Waited so long for, and were too polite to
    See we were crying,

Irony fed us: for the days we watched our
Chances to please them, nights in rumpled beds lay
Gored by their phantoms, guilty most of suffering,
    We were rewarded.

While we admired how ignorance became them,
Coldness adorned, they came at length to trust us,
Made us their mirrors: last their hopeless loves to
    Us they confided.

They were our teachers: what we are, they made us.
Cautious our converse, prudent our behaviour,
Guarded our faces: we behind them lurking,
    Greedy, devourers.

LADY HAUNTS GHOSTS

Others there are whose phantoms nightly rouse them,
Down the dark stair drive, shrinking but accustomed,
Nightlong to search where features are confounded:
    Them I must envy.

Mine are too faint: I take the whip and urge them,
Make them descend, their squeaks and wails unheeded,
Drag them like bait for lower worlds to clutch at,
    Frail, unresisting.

Back in the light I rummage them, ransack them,
Breathe them and suck them, wolfish, famished, rake for
News of my lost ones, gone where gods of darkness
    Keep, unforgiving.

WORDS FAILING

When we were young, they filched and harried for us,
Scoured on our errands lands and seas untiring,
Laboured in mines, brought treasure from the mountains,
    Eager, obedient.

Can spirits age like us? I found them weary—
Sick—hard to rouse, old spells near failing—then, like
Ghosts of the dead their faces, hands, were empty,
    Hollow their answers.

Worst is the last: their wilful, vengeful absence.
Can you forget, ungrateful, how you need me,
Now more than ever? mine the word that drags you
    Into existing.

Strangers they haunt, are drawn to others' windows.
I, drooping here, search for the word to free you,
Me too release, as—was it in a story?—
    Sins are forgiven.

TRANSACTION

Did they call us up, hoping something from us?
Or is it we, uncalled, haunt them, accusing,
Gripe like back taxes? Drawn, compelled, we find them
    Not pleased to see us.

Here at their window—who is out, who inside?—
We, as it seems to us, commence to bargain:
'Take freely what we need to give, allow it,
    Don't keep a reckoning'.

From their lit rooms, they envy us our freedom,
Not grasping how insatiable our pride, our
Will to ask nothing: each now bound the other's
    Purchase on darkness.

JUSTICE

Someone we know whose fancy runs to court scenes;
Love pleads half-choked with Knowledge his accuser;
Innocence, called to witness, faints untimely:
    'Hang him', the sentence.

Our fancies tend not that way, but to green fields,
Pastoral groves, with birdsong, shepherds piping.
Still, there are nights imagination hauls me,
    Strong-armed, with warrant,

Into a room where witnesses are summoned,
Experts are met, my words produced against me,
Facing me, standing on his bond, my lover,
    Knife, and a balance.

MASTERS AND SERVANTS

Some born unfree, the net of stars drawn round them,
Lying as tranced, grew strong on deprivation,
Gathered their forces, cast them from their bodies,
    Sent forth to labour.

Haggard and meagre, goblins and familiars,
These drudge below ground, hate the light of Heaven,
Seek always deeper pits, bright veins of venom,
    Wait for their vengeance.

Those their tranced masters, lying, watch their cells pile
Deeper in treasures coined from pain, from anger,
Spoiled love, ungiven, mined by powers who waste on
    Starvation's wages.

Too late a world that, cold, asked nothing of them,
Left them to spin creations from their bowels,
Made them enchanters, dazzled at their window
    Envies their riches.

Too soon to tell you how the story ended.
Now my magisters, articled to darkness,
Wait for the night their prison shall be rended,
    Rendered their audit.

A LOST SOUL

Some are plain lucky—we ourselves among them:
Houses with books, with gardens, all we wanted,
Work we enjoy, with colleagues we feel close to—
      Love we have, even:

True love and candid, faithful, strong as gospel,
Patient, untiring, fond when we are fretful.
Having so much, how is it that we ache for
      Those darker others?

Some days for them we could let slip the whole damn
Soft bed we've made ourselves, our friends in Heaven
Let slip away, buy back with blood our ancient
      Vampires and demons.

First loves and oldest, what names shall I call you?
Older to me than language, old as breathing,
Born with me, in this flesh: by now I know you're
      Greed, pride and envy.

Too long I've shut you out, denied acquaintance,
Favoured less barefaced vices, hoped to pass for
Reasonable, rate with those who more inclined to
      Self-hurt than murder.

You were my soul: in arrogance I banned you.
Now I recant—return, possess me, take my
Hands, bind my eyes, infallibly restore my
      Share in perdition.

COMPLICITIES

Here we are, bound to—allies, should we call them?
Awkward to label—not the least of ways they're
Tricksome, undocile, no more like our childhood's
    Shy unseen playmates.

Signed our confederates—what more's in the compact?
What's due to them is plain, but what comes our way?
Presences teasingly remindful, glances
    Hard to find friendly.

Why did we choose them: had we an intention?
Conscience—confessor—scourge—or secret witness?
What did we hope from them? are they the ones we
    Trust to betray us?

Come the great day when fuses shall be lighted,
Books come unsealed and demons be decanted,
Dark come to light—in short, be blown to blazes
    All our glass houses—

Creatures, familiars, cherished bosom-serpents,
What will their part be—catch us with the matches?
Not our concern—for us, enough to hold to:
    They shall inherit.

FAVOURITE STORY

Whose is the greatest love? the tale's magister
Saves by his mercy lover, doting lady,
Honourable lord—himself not good, not noble,
    Christendom's outcast.

Few is it given, others' bonds assuming,
Them to redeem from cumulated folly.
Well, they are paid: no greed like sacrifice, no
    Pride like sin-eaters'.

He sees in secret how the seasons ripen,
Fall turns to winter: sun is sick, then dying:
Time's gate stands open: last, to him descend the
    Murdering angels.

PALLADIA AND OTHERS

Stranger—I doubt your father was an oak-tree,
Mother a rock, nor were you dropped from heaven,
Mystic, untouchable—so like me I guess you're
       Human-descended.

Still, you call up veiled statues, secret cities,
Mazes that grant to few conditioned entry,
Ivory heights whose walls when one assails them
       Shine but prove bruising.

Too-sacred persons I've adored before you,
Crept to their shrines with painful, cautious offerings:
Under the altar found, asleep or hiding, their
       Small fuzzy brothers.

These proved approachable—you might say, playful:
Liked what was offered, showed no circumspection,
Raised no obstruction: I with them concluded
       Private arrangements.

Come, man of stone, of ivory, of glass, with
Me just this once—to this sharp brink: peer over:
See, in their hell, in perfect circle lie the
       Feeder, devourer.

HECATE TRIVIA

Here in a land of faultless four-leaved clovers,
Learning from books how, back before our windows,
Mirrors, your dusty forks were where uncanny
    Worlds faced each other,

We, where our fathers banished wolf and Indian,
Vainly regret their vanished sense and vigour:
Now in our cities take a last, last stand with
    Rat and with cockroach.

Goddess of crossways, three-faced, was it you my
Muse all this while? you are the last who hallows
Contents of pockets, broken dolls, dead puppies:
    Queen, garbage-eater.

SCAMANDER

Strangeness of water: Nature sends her streams forth
Here, and there closes—feeds, or dries for ever—
Or, sent from sight, sets free in distant places,
    Lost, but found living.

Strange powers they have: for life, death, transformation—
Flowing from desert rocks, from wounds, from insult,
Vengeance of nymphs—Salmacis' obscene waters
    Draining men's forces.

Springs of Scamander, two, one warm, one freezing,
Site now unknown: what emblem do you pose me?
No Muses' fountains, merely where the Trojans
    Carried their washing—

Springs where that hero city-holding Hector
Found gods are partial: breasts of Earth, unequal
Fates dealt to men—our place prepared a dark one, by
    Nature, false mother.

AFTER THE EXPLOSION

Now we're alone at length, my tadsome witsome,
All lids blown off, all old companions frighted,
Back to the basics—sobbing in my bed, and
    Clutching my dolly.

No-one at the window—even Nosferatu,
Weary of blood, has gone off picking daisies;
Nor at the door pleads, dank with night, the lover.
    Empty, unhaunted

Stands now my house, though cleared and swept for devils.
Meantime my garden sprouts, unhelped, unhindered.
No need to ask, death and its host departed,
    What we do after.

Let's make a grave, my ted, and put you in it,
Under the compost heap, where all things quicken.
Take with you silence—secrets: I commit us to
    Earth with her courses.

III

THE DARK SIDE

KARLOFF POEM

If you love me, take me back
To tread again the ancient track
That leads where my lost pleasures are,
The land of far Vissaria.

Always different, but the same,
Castle with the mystic name,
Stairway to the underground
Where the lost ones shall be found.

'Doctor, you can ease my pain,
Cleanse my soul and change my brain':
Seeking through the caverns wild
Where the giant led the child.

Ice may freeze them, fire may burn,
Nonetheless they shall return,
Wolfman, vampire—one is gone,
Karloff, lacy skeleton.

Take the lantern: here I'll stay,
Nevermore behold the day,
Keep a lasting watch above
My undying monster love.

IN THAT CELLAR

Where I laid my   murdered brother,
Where I laid my   angry mother,
Where I laid my   luckless sister,
        In that cellar
They lie, they lie, they lie.

Stitched with wires and   gashed with axes,
Bound with chains and   mummy-swaddled,
Eyes pricked out and   spines unthreaded,
        In that cellar
They wait, they wait, they wait.

There I lie, to   them committed,
Theirs my hope, and   theirs my patience,
Till the judgment,   till light finds us,
        In that cellar
Is all, is all, is all.

THE WELL

A winter hanging over the dark well,
My back turned to the sky,
To see if in that blackness something stirs,
Or glints, or winks an eye:

Or, from the bottom looking up, I see
Sky's white, my pupil head—
Lying with all that's lost, with all that shines—
My winter with the dead:

A well of truth, of images, of words.
Low where Orion lies
I watch the solstice pit become a stair,
The constellations rise.

ORION

Orion is the winter-king
Among heaven's bright designs.
His up is down: his height is set
In Hell, and yet he shines.

Those stars of night the fiend drew down,
That followed in his train,
At midnight stand above the town:
They glitter in their pain.

My foolstar hero, stretched at length,
The sky's pins through his head,
Basks at those fires his dreary strength
That's slanted to the dead.

Come, darkness, fill my heart and eyes:
I'll sink below the light,
And, buried with Orion, rise
To winter and to night.

THEY RETURN

Long desired, the dead return.
—Saw our candle and were safe,
Bought from darkness by our care?
Light from ours has touched their eyes,
Blood of ours has filled their veins.
Absence, winter, shed like scales.

They return, but they are changed.
Armoured each in private shade,
Sullen, helmed against the light,
Their resentment fills our arms,
Sifting from their ribs like night.
Absence, winter, is their name.

Change comes slowly, where they were.
Pain, exclusion, long endured,
Ate their human places out,
Sold to darkness by our fear.
They, returning, bring us back
Absence, winter, what we gave.

IV

RECOGNITIONS

DISCOVERY

Artless fuzzwit! was it you, then
—Infant, far from reckless teens—
Laid a powder plot, and blew the
Man of glass to smithereens?

Or, did someone—nameless, faceless—
Set you on? were you beguiled?
For such plot, my grimoires tell me,
Take a feeble-minded child.

Gentle babe, with such intentions!
Now we've seen what you could do,
Lie there, fertilize my garden:
See what earth will make of you.

Though, I never meant to lose you,
Little thorn of poison tree:
Nights I lay me down beside you,
When I wake, am still with thee.

SURROGATE

Not common wormfood, quick to rot—
An alien in the earth--
A simple ted, with nylon thread,
What should he know of birth?

Shaped from another stock than me,
Digged from a different pit,
He went before to find a door,
And he can open it.

He is the Tammuz of my song,
Of death and hell the key,
And gone to mend the primal wrong,
That rift in Being, Me.

To with my flesh explore the fire,
Or in the springs to drown,
Or seek, this late, the earthward stair
Where Tadwit hurried down,

No need: poor changeling, never born,
Stuffed brain and glassy eye,
Is planted by the spring of tears,
The first of me to die.

MESSENGER

Down he went, and found a boat
On the darkness set afloat:
Tadwit, my perduring friend,
Where will your adventures end?

Take me, guide of souls, with you,
Paddled in your ghost-canoe:
Through the waters deep and wide,
Bring me to the further side.

Shall we land where other teds
Cling all day with drowsy heads
To the eucalyptus-trees
In the far Antipodes?

Cradled on the rocking lake,
I could sleep and never wake:
Seems not my concern to know
Where my Tadwit means to go;

Nor, when once we've passed the flood,
Landed high and dry for good,
Messenger, my teddy-bear,
Shall I ask you who you were.

GATHERING IN

Angel, what about the others?
There's a Tammuz who's not you—
Trapped between two-natured mothers—
Rescue him, we need him too.

Sticklebacked and hurtful baby
Turning in the tide I saw—
Does he come with us? or maybe
Gone to spike the dragon's maw.

There's the mermaid, gaunt and bony,
Shrinking from your boathead's light,
Sister to Medusa stony—
Now's the chance to do her right.

Naked spectres, come for shrouding,
Those I failed and snubbed and crossed,
In the deadly waters crowding:
Angel, let not one be lost.

TRANSFORMATION

Tadwit is the world-tree made:
I, reposing in his shade,
See through leaves the heavens, where
Whirls in play a smallish Bear,
Bright, immortal, close and dear
As the eye's crystalline sphere.
Punished giants, monsters dim—
All the heaven turns on him.

V

SHADOWS FLEE

UMBRELLA POEM

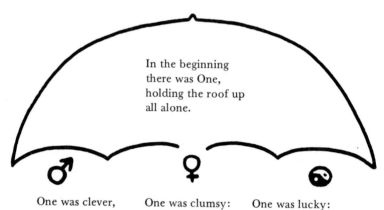

In the beginning
there was One,
holding the roof up
all alone.

One was clever,
invented Two—
nice—accepting—
joy! calloo!
—found at length it
wouldn't do—
or, more likely,
always knew
time would wear the
plaything through.

One was clumsy:
darling Two
got mislaid or
slipped from view:
haunted forest,
space, ensue.

One was lucky:
God sent Two,
with a note its
name was *You*—
magic word to
make things new!
out of One, be-
hold, *I* grew.

Rooftree—wordtree—
space—time—friend—
make some shelter,
till the end.

WHAT FALADA SAID

All I have left from home—the horse that brought me,
Dead, flayed, its head hung up, its power of speaking
Left, like an echo—gives its daily message
    In the dark entry:

'Daughter, betrayed and drudging here in exile,
Those who let these things happen were—believe me—
Foreigners, strangers, none of those who loved you:
    Not your true mother.

She if she knew would send someone to fetch you,
Carry you home, restore the past, again her
Child, joy from pain: at least, if she could know it
    She would be sorry.'

So on my nursery floor my dolls consoled me.
No: there are four, not two: a constellation
Turning: maimed child, barbed mother—torn, rent open
    Womb, bladed baby.

VISITING

Like me, you're expert in
Those upper rooms
—Intimate places,
Both lights and glooms—
Where, before cockcrow, the
Revenant comes—

Buried bride, demon king,
Treacherous guest
(Cold, and you warmed him;
Tired, you let rest:
Now there's a leaden pain
Rankling your breast).

There was that other one
You couldn't see:
Takes one to know one: he
Never fooled me,
Even without the
Blood on the key.

Likely we've both of us
Been here before,
Maybe too often: I
Can't any more
Tell you to what, love, you've
Opened your door.

SET-UPS

Who's the original
Treacherous Guest,
Promising comfort
With spikes in his vest?
Slide to the underworld,
Chute to The Pit,
Tortures of tangle
Of Him, Her & It.
Him was no problem—
You were A Fact—
But how did Mamma get
Into the act,
Lurk at the bottom,
Rocking her pain,
Cradle poor It into
Life once again?
Ladies should watch who they
Take into bed:
Pity—too late for
Me & my ted.

                    *

He told me He had come from You:
'Twas You I clutched in Him:
But half-seas-over rolled the view,
And would I need to swim?

He might report to You, I thought—
A spy, did I infer?
A friendly go-between? In court,
They showed He spied for Her.

She gave him honey, buns and tea,
Perhaps before I was,
Suborning thus my friend from Me,
As They say, just 'Because'.

If He and You were always Hers,
The friends I count are three,
Her last-appointed murderers,
Named I, Myself, and Me.

PLAYING

Let me describe to you
Life on Square One:
Surface not solid, though
Hard as a stone—
Starting-posts sprout, but there's
No clear-marked track—
I venture runs, but I'm
Always bounced back.

Can I conjecture how
Square Two might look?
Maybe some greenery—
Maybe a brook—;
Oftener it strikes me,
Likely Square Two
Never got marked on this
Board, and you knew—

Hardly a player,
Nothing to win,
Clocking how long I might
Take to clue in.
Now we've exhausted the
Charms of Square One,
Maybe you know a
Game that's some fun?

EPILOGUE

OLD AGE OF THE TEDDY-BEAR

Ted getting shabby—
skull beneath skin?
No, but as matting,
bare patches, begin,
nameless maimed baby
peers out from within.

Once it was Tadwit,
now merely It:
old links with You and Him
no longer fit:
the melting snowman's slide,
leaving just grit?

Poor ted? no—frightening,
way it seems now:
angel that shielded me
gone soft like dough:
now to that damaged thing
what do I owe?

Something in both of us
never got born:
too late to hack it out,
or to unlearn
needed, familiar pain.
Come, little thorn.

THE END

Guide to dark places—finder of lost direction—
Tearspring-diviner, and where the wordhoard lay:
Now is a blank, a thing, as dumb as its stuffing.
Magic like that runs out, it doesn't stay.
Crying I question my gods, the One, the jealous.
'I never meant you to keep it,' is what They say.

NOTES & ACKNOWLEDGEMENTS

Reader, if the names appall,
Panic's needless, after all.
'Nosferatu' is a movie,
Murnau, '22 (yes, groovy)—
Dracula without permission,
Hence the names received revision.
Homer's here, but in the light
Of A.B. Lord and Jackson Knight:
Sapphics likewise impure, stemming
From the hymn-tune known as Flemming.
Tammuz, Dumuzi, are the same
(Sorry, that's the way they came),
Babylon & Sumer versions
(Always were elusive persons—
Still, for details see J.B.
Pritchard, ed., *A N E T*).

Twenty some-odd years ago
Oxford took an ark in tow,
And thereafter never quite
Chose to let it slip from sight.
Heartfelt thanks I here express,
Bill Toye, alias Oxford Press!

This, though now in Oxford's book,
First came forth on private hook.
Friends assisted, not a few—
Bear up, Muse, we'll list just two
In a thanks-again review
(Pausing, though, to not pass over
Picture sourcebooks pub. by Dover):
Best of readers, Northrop Frye
Cast a sure arranging eye;
David Blostein, craftsman fine,
Caught, with steadier hand than mine,
Ted, glum chum, in subtle line.
Major debts thus once more noted,
Muse, let's jump: our boat's re-floated.